# They Called Me, Savage

## Savage

Amanda Neil

They Called Me, Savage © 2023 Amanda Neil

All rights reserved.

No part of this publication may be reproduced, stored in a retrieval system, or transmitted, in any form or by any means, electronic, mechanical, photocopying, recording or otherwise, without the prior written permission of the presenters.

Amanda Neil asserts the moral right to be identified as author of this work.

Presentation by *BookLeaf Publishing*

Web: www.bookleafpub.com

E-mail: info@bookleafpub.com

ISBN: 9789357442381

First edition 2023

*They Called Me, Savage is dedicated to my grandfather, William Coburn, and all of the grandfathers that came before him.*

*There's a little Savage in all of us.*

# ACKNOWLEDGEMENT

I would like to thank my mother, Pamela, because without her, this book would have never been completed. From reading drafts, giving advice on the title, and teaching me that I can be anything I want to be, even a Witch. Thank you for everything.

I must acknowledge my 10th Great-Grandfather, Thomas Morgan Carrier, he is the subject and inspiration for this book. His story deserves to be told. Thomas was an interesting man and I will not allow him to be lost to history.

Finally, I would like to thank my Grandmother Marie and my Aunt Victoria. Until we meet again.

Beannaithe Bheith

# PREFACE

This book is a collection of poetry inspired by the life and times of Thomas Morgan Carrier. Executing a king was just the beginning for Thomas and loving an accused witch was far from the end. This is the companion book to, One Of Us Is The Devil, a collection of poetry and history inspired by Martha Carrier.

The title of this book, "They Called Me, Savage" comes from a story handed down in our family. Thomas is my 10th Great-Grandfather and as the story goes, he earned the nickname Savage, by being a friend to the Native Americans, first in Massachusetts and then in Connecticut. Thomas would help them and had a reputation for being mean, ruthless even, so the nickname stuck.

They called him, Savage.

# For King and Country

A Welshman in another place and time,
A far away lifetime ago.

Mother said, "For King and Country you must
now prepare to go. For King and Country your
life is owed."

In that time, I paid dearly,
For a duty that was not my own.
To be cast away, across the sea,
To be lost in a land That I did not know.

Remembering the words,
Reciting them now,
For King and Country, your life,
Is what is owed.

Another time in another world,
A promise land awaits, I was told.
For King and Country,
And a bag of gold.

This poem was inspired by the story of how
Thomas Morgan Carrier came to the colonies,
fleeing England and the life he knew for
something he could have never imagined.

# Debt Untold

They said I'd pay,
The King has died.
I've known all this time.

Over 100 years of lives,
Bought and Sold.
There were no riches
Debt Untold.

There was no promised land.
Only strife and heartache.
No matter what life I made.

For King and Country,
I was made to believe.
My debt is paid to thee.

# Away, Away

Away, Away

To the hills we will roam

Away, Away

To my Colchester home

Away, Away

To where the sky meets the sea

Away, Away

To the castle on a foggy Welsh morn

Away, Away

To the hills we will roam

Away, Away

To my Colchester home.

# The Crown

Where our secrets are hidden
From this world we know
From the land and time
From all that is familiar
From all that I know

Where blood runs deep
From family
From shadows
To the crown that I keep

A headsman I am
For all that must know
A man has his secrets
The crown is for show

# Follow Me

Witches they say
They come in the night
They are evil and wicked
From the very first sight

But no, my child
You follow me
I will show you
The truth the others won't see

We are just the same as they
Time and time over
No matter what the evil ones say

So remember that I am you and you are me
And together we are witches
You see....

# They Called Me, Savage

They called me, Savage

You took my home

They called me, Savage

Forced to kill for you

They called me, Savage

You took my wife

My children

My home

But not my life

They called me, Savage




Might as well live up to the name….

# Demons

Forced to flee

Forced to be

Forced to carry your burdens with me

Forced to kill

Forced to try

Forced to believe all of your lies

Forced to love

Forced to hate

Forced to endure the trouble at your gates

Forced to live

Forced to fight

Forced to keep on living out of spite

Forced out of my home

Forced to be a nomad

Forced to roam

Forced to listen

Forced to be controlled

I'll be damned if I let the demons take hold.

# It Was Always You

I used to think that Spring was when time renewed.

The flowers, the birds, and the crops in the fields.

Then I realized, it was always you.

The sky, the stars, thrown onto the night sky.

Sparkling and renewed, one at a time.

It was always you.

Always has been.

It was always you.

# Now and Today

My life was my own

A man tall and strong

But my heart is broken in two

It is not my own breath

That keeps me alive

I am still broken

That may never change


Now time has left me

And come back again

Time cannot heal

My pain is renewed

For the only things

That make me smile

Are far and few

Until we meet again

In another way

Keep me with you

Always, now and today

# In The Shadows

I walk in the shadows

Where no one else dare go

I live in the shadows

So no one will know

No heart, No soul

In this body you'll find

I am the shadow

I am not alive

# She Stayed

She stayed with me

Longer than her life

She stayed with me

Guided me through

She stayed with me

She also stayed with you

She stayed through the trials and the pain

She stayed to teach you a lesson

She stayed to keep me sane

She stayed in silence

Was she really there?

She Stayed.

# My Andover Witch

My Andover Witch

You say she was evil

I think otherwise

You say she was the devil

That's you in disguise

My Andover Witch

She did nothing to thee

Nothing that wasn't deserved

You see...

My Andover Witch

She doesn't answer to you

My Andover Witch

Why do you care?

My Andover Witch

She walks with me

My Andover Witch

She helps me see

# Scars

When you take from another

It leaves a scar

In time it makes a void in life

When death is not denied

An eye for an eye

My debt is paid

For you have taken my blood

Thrown my life away

# Ghost Of My Years

I wander the paths of my life

With the ghost of my years

Gone

Knowing they will come back for me one day

And away with them I will ride

Back to the castle in Colchester

They will take me home

Back to the hills

Where I was born to roam

# Savage

Solitude

Avenging

Values

Admirable

Gracious

Elusive

# Morgan Is Me

From the tower they call

One by one

From the tower they fall

Headsman after Headsman

Taken from life

From the tower they call

For my life

Morgan, Morgan

Where is he?

Morgan is still alive

Morgan is me

I will carry Morgan for the rest of my life

Morgan lived.

Morgan survived.

# Cursed

21

Cursed to go

Cursed to flee

Cursed to carry your burden with me

Cursed to kill

Cursed to fight

Cursed to ensure

Cursed to lead

Cursed to be the man you expect me to be…..

# Magic Follows

Magic Follows

It carries seeds of doubt

Exiled and banned from Billerica, Andover, And England

Magic Follows

The good and the bad

Magic Follows

Carried across the sea

Magic Follows

Let it be

www.ingramcontent.com/pod-product-compliance
Lightning Source LLC
Chambersburg PA
CBHW071535131025
33937CB00046B/1212